Under This

Divine

Protection

Pius Joseph © Text 2020

All rights Reserved.

No part of this publication may be reproduced, distributed, or transmitted in any form or by any means, including photocopying, recording, or other electronic or mechanical methods, without the prior written permission of the publisher

Except in the case of brief quotations embodied in critical reviews and certain other noncommercial uses permitted by copyright law. The author is aware that the application of this book may differ from one person to another as such things as faith, persistence, trust, and love for God can determine the outcomes that you receive from the application of the principles in this book.

Unless otherwise indicated, all scriptural quotations are taken from the King James Version © 1988-2007 Bible Soft Inc.

Scripture marked NKJV is taken from the New King James Version®. Copyright © 1982 by Thomas Nelson. Used by permission. All rights reserved.

TABLE OF CONTENTS

TABLE OF CONTENTS	4
A WORD	8
CHAPTER 1	1
COVENANT OF DIVINE PROTECTION	1
ACTIVATING THE COVENANT OF DIVINE PROTECTION FOR YOUR HEALTH	7
BY THE BLOOD	10
GOD'S FIRE	17

SAY IT	21

CHAPTER 2 — 27

YOU ARE IN GOSHEN	27
PSALMS AND PRAYERS FOR DIVINE PROTECTION	30
PSALMS FOR DIVINE COVERING	30
A PSALM OF GOD'S PRESENCE	39
A PSALM OF GOD SALVATION FROM INFIRMITY	42
A PSALM OF GOD'S ROCK OVER YOU	46
A PSALM OF GOD'S PRESERVATION	50
A PSALM OF GREAT CONFIDENCE IN DIVINE PROTECTION	54
A PSALM OF GOD'S FAITHFULNESS FOR PAST DIVINE PROTECTION	59
A PSALM OF PROTECTION FROM BOW OF AFFLICTION	63
A PSALM OF GOD'S ASSURED PROTECTION	67

CHAPTER 3 — 71

HOW TO PROTECT YOUR FAMILY FROM INFIRMITY AND SICKNESS	71

CHAPTER 4 — 82

FEAR NOT	**82**
IMPORTANT DECISION	**88**
OUR BOOKS	**89**

A WORD

How healthy you are, and how protected you are is of great interest to you and God. Without health, it is impossible to serve God effectively. It is for this reason that God puts a hedge of protection around your life so that no sickness and disease can distract you from serving him. Without the hedge of God or divine protection, every believer on the earth is vulnerable to all conceivable attacks of the enemy.

If you are reading this book right now, and you are desiring to enjoy divine protection, you are not alone in this. While it is true that God promises to heal us of any disease that the enemy may throw against our health, he also promises to protect us from all sicknesses and diseases. Not only will God protect us, he also promises to protect all that concerns us. The devil even acknowledge the fact of God's divine protection in the life of Job. God built his wall of protection on all of Job's children from the onslaught of the devil.

You can find in this book words of encouragement, prayers and Scriptures that give you the assurance that the gates of hell doesn't prevail against you and your family.

Just as God protected the Israelites from plagues in the Bible, that is how you will be shielded from every attack of infirmity, sicknesses, diseases, or even an outbreak of disease.

As you read the pages of this book, I want your heart to be opened because the covenant of divine protection is about to be activated over your life in Jesus name.

CHAPTER 1

Covenant of Divine Protection

A covenant is an agreement between two people, which is usually ratified by the parties that they will fulfil their obligations. Often, when God enters a covenant with man, depending on the type of covenant he entered with that man, God is faithful to fulfil his own aspect of the covenant even though the man may fail.

The day that God breaches his covenant, that day, he ceases to be God. Every child of God that is born of God is supposed to enjoy the covenant of divine protection. There is supposed to be a hedge around the life of that child of God, and everything that concerns him. This covenant of divine protection is activated by a spiritual transfer process which occurs at salvation.

Colossians 1:15

> *Who hath delivered us from the power of darkness, and hath translated us into the kingdom of his dear Son:*

Why does God take interest in your divine protection?

- The attacks of the enemy
- from sickness and diseases
- from the wickedness of man

What we have listed above are some of the reasons God takes interest in protecting you.

Psalms 89:34

> *My covenant will I not break,*
> *nor alter the thing that is gone*
> *out of my lips*

It is obvious from the Scripture above that God has promised never to break the covenant of divine protection over the lives of his children.

No matter the situation and whatever the doctor may say, this is an infallible promise of God over your divine protection, and it can never be broken. Whenever God has uttered a word, it must be fulfilled even if it was a mistake. This is why the Bible says, I never alter the words that have gone out of my lips.

When Daniel decided to violate the decree which banned prayers for 30 days, the men who sought that Daniel should be cast into the lion's den reminded the King that the law of Medes and Persians, cannot be changed. They came to the king, just sign the law. Not just an ordinary law, but one made according to the principles of the Medes and Persians that once made, it can never be altered.

Daniel 6:8, 14-15

Now, O king, establish the decree, and sign the writing, that it be not changed, according to the law of the Medes and Persians, which altereth not.

14 Then the king, when he heard these words, was sore displeased with himself, and set his heart on Daniel to deliver him: and he laboured till the going down of the sun to deliver him.

15 Then these men assembled unto the king, and said unto the

> *king, Know, O king, that the law of the Medes and Persians is, That no decree nor statute which the king establisheth may be changed.*

Now, these are all mortal men that made laws that cannot be changed. If mortal men can make laws that cannot be altered, how about God who has declared that his covenant of divine protection with you will never be broken or altered.

The object of this book is not only to encourage you in times of sickness but to ensure that you will never fall sick as a result of walking in the covenant of divine protection. I want you to know the differences between the covenant of divine protection and healing over affliction. In case of healing, you are sick and you are seeking the face of the Lord for your healing. Conversely, in divine protection, you are insisting that based on the infallible promises of God, you aren't permitted to be sick.

You are simply reminding God of his words that he has spoken in the covenant of divine protection. The sickness cannot come near your dwelling which is the covenant of divine protection.

Activating the Covenant of Divine Protection for Your Health

Have you seen believers sick? Yes! Have you seen those who love God struggling with their health? Yes! Does God want them sick? No! The covenant must be activated for it to work. You can enter into an agreement with someone, and it may be written or documented. When the other person decides to breach the terms of the agreement you entered with him, it is left for you to insist that he performs his obligation or you decide to waive your right and forget about it.

If the person is becoming obstinate, you can even take the matter to the court of law. The court may order him to return your money under the contract or to specifically perform his obligation which he has promised to do.

Whenever the devil comes against your health, you should remind God of the covenant of divine protection over your life. Based on the covenant you have with God, the sickness or infirmity has no place in your life.

Isaiah 43:26

> *Put me in remembrance: let us plead together: declare thou, that thou mayest be justified.*

God knows about the covenant of divine protection, yet he says you should remind him of his promises.

How do you activate the covenant of divine protection?

By the Blood

The first time that the blood of Jesus was ever applied in the Bible was in the book of Exodus.

Exodus 12:1-13

> *And the Lord spake unto Moses and Aaron in the land of Egypt, saying,*
>
> *2 This month shall be unto you the beginning of months: it shall be the first month of the year to you.*
>
> *3 Speak ye unto all the congregation of Israel, saying, In the tenth day of this month they shall take to them every*

man a lamb, according to the house of their fathers, a lamb for an house:

4 And if the household is too little for the lamb, let him and his neighbour next unto his house take it according to the number of the souls; every man according to his eating shall make your count for the lamb.

5 Your lamb shall be without blemish, a male of the first year: ye shall take it out from the sheep, or from the goats:

6 And ye shall keep it up until the fourteenth day of the same month: and the whole assembly of the congregation of Israel shall kill it in the evening.

7 And they shall take of the blood, and strike it on the two side posts and on the upper door post of the houses, wherein they shall eat it.

8 And they shall eat the flesh in that night, roast with fire, and unleavened bread; and with bitter herbs they shall eat it.

9 Eat not of it raw, nor sodden at all with water, but roast with fire; his head with his legs, and with the purtenance thereof.

10 And ye shall let nothing of it remain until the morning; and that which remaineth of it until the morning ye shall burn with fire.

11 And thus shall ye eat it; with your loins girded, your shoes on your feet, and your staff in your hand; and ye shall eat it in haste: it is the Lord's passover.

12 For I will pass through the land of Egypt this night, and will smite all the firstborn in the land of Egypt, both man and beast; and against all the gods of Egypt I will execute judgment: I am the Lord.

13 And the blood shall be to you for a token upon the houses

> *where ye are: and when I see the blood, I will pass over you, and the plague shall not be upon you to destroy you, when I smite the land of Egypt.*

God directed the children of Israelites to slay their lambs, and the blood from the lambs was to be plastered on a conspicuous part of their doorposts. As soon as they had finished that, in the night, the angel of death passed through the land of Egypt and the firstborn of every Egyptian both man and beast were killed. The Israelites were also in Egypt although in the land of Goshen.

As the angel of death passed over the land, he didn't touch a single Israelites' house as a result of the presence of the blood of the Lamb that was slain, Jesus who was the Passover lamb. The devil can't do anything to your life as long as you have the blood of Jesus on you. He can be upset with you, but he can die of frustration because the blood is a constant reminder of the fact that he can't touch you.

If you are not saved and you are reading this book right now, I want you to pray this simple prayer so that the blood of Jesus can be activated over your life for your protection especially in these times that we are.

Lord Jesus, I come before you today. I repent of all my sins. I ask that you show me mercy. Cleanse me with the blood of Jesus and write my name in the book of life. Thank you,

Father, for saving my soul in Jesus name. Amen.

Paul the Apostle had a great understanding of scripture that is why he said in the book of Galatians 6:17:

> *From henceforth let no man trouble me: for I bear in my body the marks of the Lord Jesus.*

The mark that Paul the Apostle refers to in the book of Galatians is the mark of the blood of Jesus and no matter what disease is affecting people, that mark is a constant reminder that sickness and infirmity have no place in your life.

God's fire

Besides the blood of Jesus, another covenant that God uses to shield his people from the enemy's weapon of disease and affliction is fire. The Bible says you are wrapped in God's protective fire.

Zachariah 2:5

> *For I, saith the Lord, will be unto her a wall of fire round about, and will be the glory in the midst of her.*

I believe it is the fire that the devil saw in the life of Job that made the devil confess to God, have you not surrounded him with your hedge and everything that concerns him? Does Job serve

God for nothing? And God told the devil hey, Satan, I'm going to take that fire of protection off and you can do anything you want to do, but don't touch his life.

Job 1:9-12

> *9 "Why shouldn't he when you pay him so well?" Satan scoffed. 10 "You have always protected him and his home and his property from all harm. You have prospered everything he does-look how rich he is! No wonder he 'worships' you! 11 But just take away his wealth, and you'll see him curse you to your face!"*

12-13 And the Lord replied to Satan, "You may do anything you like with his wealth, but don't harm him physically."

(TLB)

The fire of God's protection is so intense on your life that is why even demons do not try to play with it.

Hebrews 12:29.

For our God is a consuming fire.

You see, flies like to perch on anything that attracts their attention. But have you ever seen a fly perching on hot barbecue meat that is on the fire? That fly will never try it knowing full well that he may be barbecued with the meat he wants to perch on. So the fly just avoids it.

That is what the fire of God does to the enemy. If any devil wants to be roasted alive, they can go and try the fire of God's divine protection around your life. The devil will be consumed with destruction. This is why even the devil had to go and seek permission from God so that he could touch the life of Job. The fire of God's divine protection that he has kept around your life, is to keep the devil off. The devil will only be watching in frustration while you go about your normal business.

How do you activate the covenant of God's divine protection of fire? Be conscious of what you carry. Even if a disease or outbreak is raging close to you. You should ensure that the fire has not been quenched or the integrity of your hedge has not been breached. If you know that it is intact, then fear nothing. You are too precious to God to be wasted. If God raised you, protected you all this while, it is not for you to be cut short before your time by an outbreak, sickness, or infirmity. God is not a waster of eternal resources. Will you be happy if you spent all your resources building a home just for someone to come and use a day to pull it down? In the same way, God will not raise you for a common disease to come and destroy your life.

Say it

Your mouth is a weapon. You've got to use it judiciously and beneficially for your health. You need to talk. The diseases and sicknesses that come to confront your life are spirits. They can hear and they can listen. The Bible calls it the spirit of infirmity and diseases.

Luke 13:11

> *And, behold, there was a woman which had a spirit of infirmity eighteen years, and was bowed together, and could in no wise lift up herself.*

And do spirits hear, yes they do? Do spirits talk yes they do.

Matthew 8: 28-32

And when he was come to the other side into the country of the Gergesenes, there met him two possessed with devils, coming out of the tombs, exceeding fierce, so that no man might pass by that way

29 And, behold, they cried out, saying, What have we to do with thee, Jesus, thou Son of God? art thou come hither to torment us before the time?

30 And there was a good way off from them an herd of many swine feeding.

31 So the devils besought him, saying, If thou cast us out, suffer us to go away into the herd of swine.

32 And he said unto them, Go. And when they were come out, they went into the herd of swine: and, behold, the whole herd of swine ran violently down a steep place into the sea, and perished in the waters.

See what happened in this Scripture.

- The spirits recognised Jesus.
- They spoke to Jesus.
- They pleaded with Jesus to cast them into the herd of swine.

In the Bible, Jesus spoke to spirits several times to depart from the lives of people, and whenever the spirit leave a human body, the person becomes healed.

You speak the word of God concerning the covenant of divine protection and all these spirits that came to assault your life would leave. And if the Devils can't stay in your life, diseases and infirmity can't be present also.

And whenever you speak, God does exactly what you have decreed.

Numbers 14:28

Say to them,'As I live,' says the Lord, 'just as you have spoken in My hearing, so I will do to you:

(NKJV)

CHAPTER 2

You Are in Goshen

Exodus 8:22-23

> *22 And I will sever in that day the land of Goshen, in which my people dwell, that no swarms of flies shall be there; to the end thou mayest know that I am the Lord in the midst of the earth.*

> *23 And I will put a division between my people and thy people: to morrow shall this sign be.*

Goshen isn't just a city, but a place in Christ Jesus. I need to make this clear at the beginning of this subhead so that you understand what we are dealing with. God told Pharaoh that I will make a difference between your land and the place where my people are dwelling. Interestingly, Goshen was in the same city and very close to the place where the Egyptians were dwelling. The Israelites were living in Goshen. Yet none of the plagues of Egypt came close to them. Our dwelling is in Christ Jesus, and as we remain in him, none of the outbreaks or sicknesses that waste the lives of people will ever affect us.

The Bible says we are seated in the heavenly places in Christ Jesus.

Ephesians 2:6

> *And hath raised us up together, and made us sit together in heavenly places in Christ Jesus:*

We are far beyond the reach of the spirit of infirmity and diseases. The only way that sicknesses and diseases can affect us, is when they can reach the heavenly places where we are seated with Christ Jesus.

The Bible says we are hidden in Christ and Christ in God. Before the devil can get to you, he must overcome God, overcome Christ, And Then he meets you.

Psalms and Prayers for Divine Protection

Psalms for Divine Covering

Reflection

Psalm 91: 1-16

> *He that dwelleth in the secret place of the most High shall abide under the shadow of the Almighty.*

2 I will say of the Lord, He is my refuge and my fortress: my God; in him will I trust.

3 Surely he shall deliver thee from the snare of the fowler, and from the noisome pestilence.

4 He shall cover thee with his feathers, and under his wings shalt thou trust: his truth shall be thy shield and buckler.

5 Thou shalt not be afraid for the terror by night; nor for the arrow that flieth by day;

6 Nor for the pestilence that walketh in darkness; nor for the destruction that wasteth at noonday.

7 A thousand shall fall at thy side, and ten thousand at thy right hand; but it shall not come nigh thee.

8 Only with thine eyes shalt thou behold and see the reward of the wicked.

9 Because thou hast made the Lord, which is my refuge, even the most High, thy habitation;

10 There shall no evil befall thee, neither shall any plague come nigh thy dwelling.

11 For he shall give his angels charge over thee, to keep thee in all thy ways.

12 They shall bear thee up in their hands, lest thou dash thy foot against a stone.

13 Thou shalt tread upon the lion and adder: the young lion and the dragon shalt thou trample under feet.

14 Because he hath set his love upon me, therefore will I deliver him: I will set him on high, because he hath known my name.

15 He shall call upon me, and I will answer him: I will be with him in trouble; I will deliver him, and honour him.

16 With long life will I satisfy him, and shew him my salvation.

Holy Father, I thank you for your covering and covenant of divine protection which has assured me that I won't be wasted before my due time upon the earth. I praise your name Lord in the name of Jesus.

Heavenly Father, as I abide under your shadow, I am exempted from any disease, or sickness released by the devil against the entire world, my life, and destiny in the name of Jesus.

Glorious Father, I thank you because I am already delivered completely from every attack of outbreak of infirmity or sickness against my life in the name of Jesus.

Righteous Father, I declare that I am covered under the shadow of your wings against all outbreak and sicknesses in the name of Jesus.

Glorious Father, you said in your word that you shall be my shield and my buckler. By that same truth of the word of God, I and my family are shielded from every outbreak and infirmity in the name of Jesus.

Holy Father, I stand by the authority of your word, and I cast out every fear that is caused by the spirit of infirmity in the name of Jesus.

Gracious Father, no matter how strong an infirmity or sickness is, I am untouchable by it in the name of Jesus.

Holy Father, thank you for your sure word of the covenant of divine protection which you have uttered to me. Even if a thousand shall fall by my left, and ten thousand by my right, no infirmity or disease shall affect me or my family or those who are connected, related, or associated with me in the name of Jesus.

Heavenly Father, even though I may continue to hear about diseases and rumours of infirmities, none of it shall come near me or my family in the name of Jesus.

Glorious Father, thank you because you have committed by your word that no evil shall befall me including infirmities, diseases and all forms of sicknesses in the name of Jesus.

Heavenly Father, I praise you for your holy covenant of divine protection which you have made for me and added it with a charge or commandment to your angels to keep me and my family from all attacks of infirmity. I thank you Mighty Father for the charge given to the angels today to keep me protected from destructive missiles of sicknesses in the name of Jesus.

Glorious Father, no matter how exposed I become to any disease, it won't harm me because you have said that I will trade upon lion and adder, the young lion and dragon, but nothing shall happen to me in the name of Jesus.

Holy Father, I worship you because I am heavily defended by your love that is upon me in the name of Jesus.

Glorious Father, thank you, Lord, because I call upon you at this hour of need, and you have answered me.

Holy Father, I praise you because no infirmity or disease can waste the precious life that you have given me. You shall satisfy me with long life and show me your great salvation in the name of Jesus.

I praise you for listening to me Lord, in Jesus name.

A Psalm of God's presence

Psalm 23:1-6

> *The Lord is my shepherd; I shall not want.*
>
> *2 He maketh me to lie down in green pastures: he leadeth me beside the still waters.*
>
> *3 He restoreth my soul: he leadeth me in the paths of righteousness for his name's sake.*
>
> *4 Yea, though I walk through the valley of the shadow of*

death, I will fear no evil: for thou art with me; thy rod and thy staff they comfort me.

5 Thou preparest a table before me in the presence of mine enemies: thou anointest my head with oil; my cup runneth over.

6 Surely goodness and mercy shall follow me all the days of my life: and I will dwell in the house of the Lord for ever.

I worship and adore you for being my shepherd. I praise you because you are the only shepherd who lays down his life for your sheep. Be praise Lord in the name of Jesus.

Heavenly Father, you have said in your word that you are my shepherd, therefore, I can't want. I will never want in health in the name of Jesus.

Holy Father, I praise your name because you are the restorer of my soul. Restore my soul to your peace in the name of Jesus.

Glorious Father, however, bad the attacks of the enemy become, I refused to be afraid of any infirmity, sickness, or arrow of destruction that the enemy has unleashed against me and my family in the name of Jesus.

Glorious Father, I glorify your name because you are with me. And where ever your presence is, there is liberty and protection. I pray that the defence that follows your presence keeps me protected from all the onslaught of darkness against my health in the name of Jesus.

Holy Father, let your oil of divine protection cover me now in the name of Jesus.

Heavenly Father, cause your goodness and your mercies to rest upon me and let that goodness keep me from all the attacks of the devil against my health in the name of Jesus.

A Psalm of God Salvation from Infirmity

Psalms 20:1-9

> *The Lord hear thee in the day of trouble; the name of the God of Jacob defend thee;*

2 Send thee help from the sanctuary, and strengthen thee out of Zion;

3 Remember all thy offerings, and accept thy burnt sacrifice; Selah.

4 Grant thee according to thine own heart, and fulfil all thy counsel.

5 We will rejoice in thy salvation, and in the name of our God we will set up our banners: the Lord fulfil all thy petitions.

6 Now know I that the Lord saveth his anointed; he will hear him from his holy heaven with the saving strength of his right hand.

7 Some trust in chariots, and some in horses: but we will remember the name of the Lord our God.

8 They are brought down and fallen: but we are risen, and stand upright.

9 Save, Lord: let the king hear us when we call.

Holy Father, I make demands for the defence that is upon the name of the God of Jacob to cover me now in the name of Jesus.

Heavenly Father, I praise you today because you have always heard my prayers and supplication against all infirmities in the name of Jesus.

Glorious Father, by your mercies and grace, remember my offerings and sacrifice and keep me divinely protected in the name of Jesus.

Oh Lord, send your help to me and let me be strengthened in all areas of my life against the fear of infirmity and sicknesses in the name of Jesus.

Righteous Father, you have said in your word that you will grant me my heart desire. My heart desires is to enjoy the covenant of divine protection all the days of my life and my family in the name of Jesus.

Holy Father, I rejoice in your salvation and that will raise a banner of divine protection over me in the name of Jesus.

Holy Father, thank you for the assurances of your word that you will save all your anointed ones in the name of Jesus.

Glorious Father, I trust in your name as my shield and buckler. Some trust in chariots, bank account, their health insurance, but my trust is in your name and you will never put me to shame in the name of Jesus.

A Psalm of God's Rock over You

Reflection

Psalms 61:1-8

Hear my cry, O God; attend unto my prayer.

2 From the end of the earth will I cry unto thee, when my heart is overwhelmed: lead me to the rock that is higher than I.

3 For thou hast been a shelter for me, and a strong tower from the enemy.

4 I will abide in thy tabernacle for ever: I will trust in the covert of thy wings. Selah.

5 For thou, O God, hast heard my vows: thou hast given me the heritage of those that fear thy name.

6 Thou wilt prolong the king's life: and his years as many generations.

7 He shall abide before God for ever: O prepare mercy and truth, which may preserve him.

8 So will I sing praise unto thy name for ever, that I may daily perform my vows.

I worship you for your faithfulness to me. You hear my cries that come to you and attend to all of my supplications. Be glorified Lord in the name of Jesus.

Heavenly Father, you have declared in your word that you are the rock that is higher than I. I make demands that the **Rock** that is higher than I, will keep me divinely protected in the name of Jesus.

Holy Father, thank you for being my shelter and my strong tower from all the forces of darkness that want me sick with the spirit of infirmity in the name of Jesus.

Glorious Father, I hide under the cover of your wings and there shall I abide forever. By the reason of that cover, no infirmity or sickness shall come near me in the name of Jesus.

Holy Father, I make demands for the heritage of all those who fear your name to manifest now in my life in the name of Jesus.

Glorious Father, I pray that your mercy and your truth shall establish your divine protection over me in the name of Jesus.

Holy Father, I will sing praises to your name forever for your banner of divine protection that you have placed over me in the name of Jesus.

A Psalm of God's Preservation

Reflection

Psalm 121:1-8

> *I will lift up mine eyes unto the hills, from whence cometh my help.*

2 My help cometh from the Lord, which made heaven and earth.

3 He will not suffer thy foot to be moved: he that keepeth thee will not slumber.

4 Behold, he that keepeth Israel shall neither slumber nor sleep.

5 The Lord is thy keeper: the Lord is thy shade upon thy right hand.

6 The sun shall not smite thee by day, nor the moon by night.

7 The Lord shall preserve thee from all evil: he shall preserve thy soul.

8 The Lord shall preserve thy going out and thy coming in from this time forth, and even for evermore.

I worship and adore your name for my eyes are up. I am not looking up to the government. I'm not looking onto my doctor or the strength of the army of my country. I know that all these are means by which you can use to protect me if you desire. My eyes are lifted to your hills where my help comes from for my divine protection in the name of Jesus.

Heavenly Father, I am full of awe for you because you will never allow me to be moved by anything that the enemy does knowing full well that you are my defender.

Glorious Father, you keep me you don't slumber. Therefore, I refused to be worried over anything that the devil does in the name of Jesus.

Heavenly Father, I bless your name because you are my keeper and you always offer me a shade of divine protection against all the works of darkness which rages against my health in the name of Jesus.

Gracious Father, you have said in your word that the sun shall not smite me by day nor moon by night. No affliction or disease shall come upon me whether by day or night or any moment of human existence in the name of Jesus.

Heavenly Father, I praise your name for the assurances of your word that you will preserve me from all evil in the name of Jesus.

Holy Father, I praise you for the preservation of my going out and coming in. You are faithful to the covenant that you have spoken over my life in the name of Jesus.

A Psalm of Great Confidence in Divine Protection

Psalm 62:1-12

> *Truly my soul waiteth upon God: from him cometh my salvation.*

2 He only is my rock and my salvation; he is my defence; I shall not be greatly moved.

3 How long will ye imagine mischief against a man? ye shall be slain all of you: as a bowing wall shall ye be, and as a tottering fence.

4 They only consult to cast him down from his excellency: they delight in lies: they bless with their mouth, but they curse inwardly. Selah.

5 My soul, wait thou only upon God; for my expectation is from him.

6 He only is my rock and my salvation: he is my defence; I shall not be moved.

7 In God is my salvation and my glory: the rock of my strength, and my refuge, is in God.

8 Trust in him at all times; ye people, pour out your heart before him: God is a refuge for us. Selah.

9 Surely men of low degree are vanity, and men of high degree are a lie: to be laid in the balance, they are altogether lighter than vanity.

10 Trust not in oppression, and become not vain in robbery: if riches increase, set not your heart upon them.

11 God hath spoken once; twice have I heard this; that power belongeth unto God.

12 Also unto thee, O Lord, belongeth mercy: for thou renderest to every man according to his work.

I praise you, Father because they that wait upon God shall never be put to shame. I adore your name for the salvation of preservation is upon me.

Holy Father, I give you all the praise, and I know that no mischief of the devil or man can work against me or my family in the name of Jesus.

Heavenly Father, as I wait on you, the expectation of my divine protection shall come to pass in the name of Jesus.

Righteous Father, thank you for being my refuge, my rock, my salvation, and my defence 24-hours in the name of Jesus.

Holy Father, my entire trust is in you, and I can never be moved into any sickness or affliction in the name of Jesus.

Glorious Father, I reject every form of oppression against my health and the health of my family in the name of Jesus.

Thank you, father, for your mercy and your grace that is constantly upon me in the name of Jesus.

A Psalm of God's Faithfulness for past Divine Protection

Reflection

Psalms 44:1-10

> *We have heard with our ears, O God, our fathers have told us, what work thou didst in their days, in the times of old.*
>
> *2 How thou didst drive out the heathen with thy hand, and plantedst them; how thou didst afflict the people, and cast them out.*
>
> *3 For they got not the land in possession by their own sword,*

neither did their own arm save them: but thy right hand, and thine arm, and the light of thy countenance, because thou hadst a favour unto them.

4 Thou art my King, O God: command deliverances for Jacob.

5 Through thee will we push down our enemies: through thy name will we tread them under that rise up against us.

6 For I will not trust in my bow, neither shall my sword save me.

7 But thou hast saved us from our enemies, and hast put them to shame that hated us.

8 In God we boast all the day long, and praise thy name for ever. Selah.

9 But thou hast cast off, and put us to shame; and goest not forth with our armies.

10 Thou makest us to turn back from the enemy: and they which hate us spoil for themselves.

I praise you for your wonderful works of divine protection which I have seen and heard. You are a faithful God because if you have done it in the time past, you are capable of doing it again and again in the name of Jesus.

Holy Father, I adore your name the giver of all things who made the children of Israel obtain their inheritance not by their sword, the strength of their arm, you are worthy of all praises in the name of Jesus.

Thank you, father, for being a faithful God that you have been always to me. You have always been my banner of divine protection in the name of Jesus.

Heavenly Father, by the same hand that delivered the land of inheritance to the Israelites without fighting for it, I make demands for that same arm to raise divine protection over me in the name of Jesus.

Holy Father, I pray that your mighty arm will bring deliverance to me when my divine protection has been attacked in the name of Jesus.

Heavenly Father, I do not put my trust in my power and might. I trust you all day long for my divine protection from all infirmities in the name of Jesus.

Thank you, Lord because you will never put me to shame in the name of Jesus.

A Psalm of Protection from Bow of Affliction

Reflection

Psalm 64:1-10

Hear my voice, O God, in my prayer: preserve my life from fear of the enemy.

2 Hide me from the secret counsel of the wicked; from the insurrection of the workers of iniquity:

3 Who whet their tongue like a sword, and bend their bows to shoot their arrows, even bitter words:

4 That they may shoot in secret at the perfect: suddenly do they shoot at him, and fear not.

5 They encourage themselves in an evil matter: they commune of laying snares privily; they say, Who shall see them?

6 They search out iniquities; they accomplish a diligent search: both the inward thought of every one of them, and the heart, is deep.

7 But God shall shoot at them with an arrow; suddenly shall they be wounded.

8 So they shall make their own tongue to fall upon themselves: all that see them shall flee away.

9 And all men shall fear, and shall declare the work of God; for they shall wisely consider of his doing.

10 The righteous shall be glad in the Lord, and shall trust in him; and all the upright in heart shall glory.

Holy Father, by the virtue of the promise of your word, I reject every fear of the spirit of infirmity in the name of Jesus.

Heavenly Father, every secret counsel of the wicked against my divine protection, I frustrate it right now in the name of Jesus.

Holy Father, all plans of the enemy to shoot arrows of infirmities, afflictions, sicknesses, and outbreak against my life and the life of my family, those arrows are sent back to the sender in the name of Jesus.

Thank you, Father, because of your divine protection upon my life, many will see it, and give glory and honour to your name in the name of Jesus.

A Psalm of God's Assured Protection

Reflection

Psalms 124:1-8

> *If it had not been the Lord who was on our side, now may Israel say;*

2 If it had not been the Lord who was on our side, when men rose up against us:

3 Then they had swallowed us up quick, when their wrath was kindled against us:

4 Then the waters had overwhelmed us, the stream had gone over our soul:

5 Then the proud waters had gone over our soul.

6 Blessed be the Lord, who hath not given us as a prey to their teeth.

7 Our soul is escaped as a bird out of the snare of the fowlers:

> *the snare is broken, and we are escaped.*
> *8 Our help is in the name of the Lord, who made heaven and earth.*

Holy Father, my soul is lifted to you for protection and shield. Therefore, I can never be ashamed of the confidence I have in you in the name of Jesus.

Glorious Father, I make demands for your hand of deliverance to keep me from all evils in the name of Jesus.

Holy Father, I make demands for your salvation to keep me under divine protection in the name of Jesus.

Gracious Father, you have said in your word that the enemy cannot triumph over me. By your holy decree in that Psalm, no weapon of the enemy shall prevail against my divine protection in the name of Jesus.

Holy Father, let your mercy be ever available for me for my divine protection, in the name of Jesus.

CHAPTER 3

How to Protect Your Family from Infirmity and Sickness

When the enemy has tried all efforts to get you, but he couldn't he may change his attacks to your family. We all came from a family, and we often have a deep share of connection with where we came from. If the enemy tries to get you with the spirit of infirmity but failed, he may attack your family due to the connection which you share with them.

Often, we are saddened by what happened to the members of our family because of the connection we have with them. If your kids are sick, indirectly you are also sick. Whenever your husband or wife is suffering from an infirmity, you are also affected. In each of these cases, you may be required to become a caregiver to the sick and your daily life will be obstructed and so does your social life. Which is why you must learn to pray for your family and shield them from all the arrows of sicknesses and diseases that the enemy may direct at them. God is always willing to listen to our prayers that concern our loved ones if only we could pray them. God is also aware that we came from a family. He knows that when our family is affected in one form or the other, our service to him would be affected also.

The situation that is confronting your loved ones may become a source of major distraction or an inroad for the enemy to use against your service to God.

God doesn't need your whole family to pray before he could answer and protect your loved ones. If the whole family is praying, then that is good. But even one member of the family is enough. Someone has to be praying.

Ezekiel 22:30

And I sought for a man among them, that should make up the hedge, and stand in the gap before me for the land, that I should not destroy it: but I found none.

The Scripture above captures a powerful truth about praying out all sorts of attacks against a group of people. The Scripture says God is looking for one man. He doesn't need so many, although if so many come, he can still use them. But just one man in the family, if he finds that man, he makes a hedge with that man and through the prayers of that individual, all satanic missiles are intercepted and destroyed.

And I am glad to tell you, reading this book right now that you can be that man for your family, county or even for your whole state. You are that man that the Lord wants to use for the hedge of your family, kids, husband, wife, et cetera. You don't have to fear that you are alone. The Bible admonishes us that the one with God is the majority. You are surely on the winning side.

The devil might have been operating freely in your family because you haven't accepted the spiritual responsibility of intercession. If you can stand in the gap, all the infirmity that you see will be over. May the Lord give you that grace in the name of Jesus.

God requires your prayers for your family, wife, your kids, and your husband to ban the activities of Satan or his works. Right now I'm going to refer you to a popular Scripture that we often quote that says, if my people who are called by my name will humble themselves and pray, I will hear from heaven and heal their land (2 Chronicles 7:14). Your family is that land and I want you to accept your spiritual responsibility and pray.

Will you?

Reflection

Psalms 106:23

> *Therefore he said that he would destroy them, had not Moses*

> *his chosen stood before him in the breach, to turn away his wrath, lest he should destroy them.*

Jeremiah 5:1

> *Run ye to and fro through the streets of Jerusalem, and see now, and know, and seek in the broad places thereof, if ye can find a man, if there be any that executeth judgment, that seeketh the truth; and I will pardon it.*

Holy Father, thank you for awakening me to the spiritual responsibility of raising prayers all the time for my family to you be all the glory in the name of Jesus.

Heavenly Father, give me the grace to be a prayer warrior over the lives of my family, my neighbourhood, and my county in the name of Jesus.

Gracious Father, I make demands for the grace and the spirit of intercession to come upon me right now in the name of Jesus.

Righteous Father, as I make myself available to pray as that one man who stands in the gap for my family, neighbourhood, and my county, I ask that your shield of divine protection will be upon me in the name of Jesus.

Holy Father, I bring my entire family under the cover of the blood of Jesus.

Righteous Father, every arrow of infirmity and sicknesses that the enemy has fired into my family, my neighbourhood, I returned those arrows to where they came from in the name of Jesus.

Heavenly Father, I nullify every plan of the devil to release the spirit of infirmity against any member of my family in the name of Jesus.

Glorious Father, I pray for (mention the name of the family member that is suffering from infirmity) that your healing would come upon them right now in the name of Jesus.

Holy Father, no destruction is permitted to come against any member of my family because you have said in your word that the land cannot be destroyed once someone is standing in the gap in the name of Jesus.

Righteous Father, I reject every incantation, I reject every plan of the enemy against the health of the members of my family in the name of Jesus.

Glorious Father, I refused to allow the devil to use the infirmity or sicknesses of any member of my family as a source of distraction to me in the name of Jesus.

Thank you Holy Father because I know that your word is true and all of your promises are ye and amen. By the reason of all the promises that are contained in your word, my family is divinely protected against all the attacks of the enemy in this hour in the name of Jesus.

Thank you, Father, because this is the confidence I have in you that when I come before you with any prayer supplication or request, you always hear me. To you be all the glory and honour for granting all of my requests and petitions in the name of Jesus.

CHAPTER 4

Fear Not

The devil knows that what we fear, we will attract. Even if that thing isn't a reality now, it will become our reality sooner or later. So he spreads the spirit of fear. Once fear is there, faith is gone. Whenever you begin to notice a particular type of fear, then the devil wants to make that thing you fear a reality in your life. If you begin to fear cancer, then the spirit of cancer is around. If you begin to fear migraine headache, the spirit of migraine headache is around. But he can't just penetrate your life until you give him space through fear. To enter into your life, he brings it to your mind and then day and night, he plays the fear in your heart.

He plays the picture of the fear in your mind, once you accept it, it will become your reality. Just as job has said, "***for the thing which I greatly feared is come upon me, and that which I was afraid of is come unto me***" (Job 3: 25)

The devil knows that if we fear, infirmity must come. So before introducing his infirmity, he first sends the spirit of fear. But we can overcome that through the blood of Jesus and taking our authority, binding the spirit of fear.

Fear is one of the major instruments of the devil when it comes to oppression. He knows that when people are afraid, their fear will become a negative testimony for their lives. Fear is a spirit and it is your responsibility as a believer in Jesus Christ to bind that demon of fear. Make up your mind not to be afraid of every attack that the enemy throws at you of fear. Fear isn't of God, fear is of the devil. So bind it.

Reflection

2 Tim 1:7

> *For God hath not given us the spirit of fear; but of power, and of love, and of a sound mind.*

1 John 4:18

> *There is no fear in love; but perfect love casteth out fear: because fear hath torment. He that feareth is not made perfect in love.*

Holy Father, every spirit of fear that has been released against my life and the life of my family, I bind the spirit now in the name of Jesus.

Heavenly Father, you have said in your word that you have not given unto us the spirit of fear but of power, love, and a sound mind. By the authority that is in your word, I curse every spirit of fear out of my life and out of the life of my family in the name of Jesus.

Holy Father, every fear that I have for any disease, infirmity or even an outbreak, that wants to become my reality as a result of the consequences of fear, I reject that from becoming my reality in the name of Jesus.

Righteous Father, every grip of the spirit of fear that is upon my life right now, it is loosed by the power in the blood of Jesus.

Holy Father, I surround my life with the fire of God against all fears in the name of Jesus.

Heavenly Father, whatever infirmity that the enemy is preparing to attack me with or members of my family, and he has already started sending the fear of that infirmity, I reject it right now in the name of Jesus.

Holy Father, let your hedge of protection be upon my entire family in the name of Jesus.

Gracious Father, you said in your word that I should resist the devil steadfastly and he shall flee. I resist all spirits of fear of infirmities released against my life and the life of my family in the name of Jesus. I command them to flee and return no more in the name of Jesus.

Thank you Holy Father because the spirit of fear shall no longer have any form of expression with its consequences in my life or the life of my family in the name of Jesus.

Thank you Mighty Father for hearing and answering all of my prayers to you be all the glory and honour in the mighty name of Jesus.

Important Decision

If you are reading this book and you are not saved, pray this prayer after me:

Lord Jesus, I come before you today. I give you my heart. I give you my all. Come into my life. Become my Lord and saviour. Deliver me from the power of sin. Help me to live for you forever, in Jesus name.

Prayer

Let us know about your prayer needs as our team add you to our prayer list and intercede fervently on your behalf.

Also, check our blog for Holy Ghost inspired content.

www.thetentofglory.com

I would love to hear from you how our ministry and our books have blessed you. Write to us at

pius@thetentofglory.com

Our Books

1. The Courts of Heaven: Prayers that Open the Courts of Heaven for Healing and Deliverance

2. Powerful Prayers for Your Adult Children: How to Pray for Your Children and Secure their Future

3. Praying for My Future Husband:How to Pray for Your Husband and Enjoy A Godly Marriage

4. Praying God's Promises to Reality: Simple Ways of Praying the Promises of God for Victory & Breakthrough

5. God Wants You Protected From Disease

6. Under His Divine Protection

7. 7 Day Fasting Challenge That Will Change Your Life Forever: 7 Powerful Prayers to Pray in 7 Days

8. Praying Through the Book of Psalms for Financial Miracle: The Financial Miracle Prayer for Breakthrough

9. Burning Evil Garments: Prayers That Destroy Evil Garments, Deliverance, Breakthroughs And God's Favour Into Your Life

10. 30 Days with the Holy Spirit: Powerful Prayers and Devotional for Personal Connection with the Holy Spirit and Be His Friend

11. Breaking Evil Altars: Prayers, Decrees, Declarations for Dismantling Evil Altars

12. How to see the Supernatural: Powerful Prayers that open the Unseen Realm

13. Breaking the Spell of Disfavour: Prayers Declarations and Decrees

14. Deliverance from Shame and Reproach: Prayers, Declarations for Victory

15. Prayers that Destroy Infirmities & Diseases: Powerful Prayers that bring Healing to the Sick

16. Courtroom Prayers: Prayers And Declarations in the Courts of Heaven For

Victory, Breakthrough, and Deliverance (Free E-Book

17. How to make the Holy Ghost Your Closest Friend (Book 2) (Free-Ebook)

18. The Keys to Fervent Prayer: The Prayer Warrior Guide to Praying Always

19. Interpretation of Tongues: Be Filled with the Spirit, Unlock Speaking in Tongues & Know What You Are Praying

20. Deliverance from negative Dreams and Nightmares by Force

21. How to Build a Life of Personal Devotion to God (Free-Ebook)

22. The Holy Spirit Friendship Manual: How to make the Holy Ghost Your Close Friend (Free-Ebook)

23. Walking in the Path of Divine Direction Always

24. The Expediency of Tongues

25. Breaking Soul Ties the Simple Way: How to Break Soul Ties and Receive Freedom

26. How to Read the Bible And Understand It

27. BAPTISM OF THE HOLY SPIRIT: Easy Steps to be Filled With the Holy Spirit And Obtain the Gifts of the Holy Spirit

28. Prayer That Never Fails

29. Vision from The Heavenly

30. Baptism of the Holy Ghost Prayer Book: How to Minister the Baptism of the Holy Ghost to yourself and others.

31. How to Hear God's Voice: A Believer's Manual For Talking with God

32. Guide to Effective Fasting and Praying: A Way of Fasting And Prayers That Guarantee Results

Pius Joseph

Under His Divine Protection

Pius Joseph

Printed in Great Britain
by Amazon